Wishing you joy in your new vocation as grandparents!

To

Kate & Sean

With love from

Brian & Catherine xx

Date

Feb. 2013

Prayers *and* Promises *for* My Little Grandchild

Jerry Cook

paintings by LAURIE SNOW HEIN

HARVEST HOUSE PUBLISHERS

EUGENE, OREGON

Prayers and Promises for My Little Grandchild

Text copyright © 2012 by Jerry Cook
Paintings copyright © by Laurie Snow Hein / Courtesy of Artworks! Licensing, LLC

Published by Harvest House Publishers
Eugene, Oregon 97402
www.harvesthousepublishers.com

ISBN 978-0-7369-4326-0

Design and production by Koechel Peterson & Associates, Inc, Minneapolis, Minnesota

Unless otherwise indicated, all Scripture quotations are taken from the *Holy Bible,* New Living Translation, copyright © 1996, 2004. Used by permission of Tyndale House Publishers, Inc., Wheaton, IL 60189 USA. All rights reserved. Verses marked NIV are taken from The Holy Bible, *New International Version® NIV®*. Copyright © 1973, 1978, 1984, 2011 by Biblica, Inc.™ Used by permission. All rights reserved worldwide.

Printed in China

12 13 14 15 16 17 18 19 20 / FC / 10 9 8 7 6 5 4 3 2 1

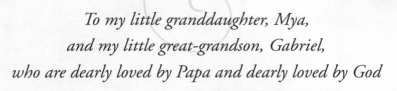

To my little granddaughter, Mya,
and my little great-grandson, Gabriel,
who are dearly loved by Papa and dearly loved by God

Now devote your heart and
soul to seeking the LORD your God.

1 Chronicles 22:19 NIV

CONTENTS

God Made Things Beautiful

It was eleven o'clock at night when the sky suddenly exploded with undulating waves of indescribable color. We stopped the car and ran to an open field beside the road. We had seen the northern lights (aurora borealis) before but nothing like this. It was a light show that demanded the entire sky as its stage. Three grown men were instantly reduced to children standing wide-eyed with wonder. No human hand could reproduce this. Here was a magnificent production, a gift freely given to anyone willing to let his tired night be interrupted by unexpected beauty.

As grandparents we must never grow so old, tired, or dull that we cannot be interrupted—at times even invaded—by the beautiful. As we grow old, we must also grow young. This is one of the gifts of grandchildren. They barge into the old and tired to bring something young and vital. They see the world as brand-new, whereas until them we'd been watching it grow a little worn and lose its luster.

Not only can we see new and young through their eyes, we must help them see the beautiful through our older, more experienced eyes. Our awe and delight in the beautiful will help them look more carefully and discover more deeply. From us they can learn that God makes things beautiful just for us to enjoy. His beauty can make us jump out of a car in the middle of the night, stumble over a fence, and run into a field to watch Him paint the sky in colors only He could conceive of and set the sky dancing in ways only He could choreograph.

HEAVENLY FATHER,

Help me hold the hands and hearts of my grandchildren.
Teach me how to awaken in them the awe of Your glory
intruding into their lives. Help them understand that
You make things beautiful just for us and that You give
us a special gift, the ability to stand transfixed, caught in
the wonder that only Your hand can create. Lord, let me
mirror for them a life easily interrupted by the beautiful.
Help us walk together in awe. Amen.

The heavens declare the glory of God;
the skies proclaim the work of his hands.
PSALM 19:1 NIV

7

God's Special Creation

I'm convinced that grandchildren are the most wonderful gifts a grandparent could ever receive. They are not only precious to us; they are precious to God. I want them to know they didn't just happen. They didn't evolve from some hairy creature. They aren't just another animal romping around on an accidental planet with no particular purpose other than to romp around.

The Bible tells us how God created everything. In the book of Genesis, a wonderful story portrays God carefully sculpting a beautiful work of art. When it is finally finished and perfect in His eyes, He leans forward and breathes—literally kisses—it to life. No longer is there an *it*. Now there is a *him*. And later He creates a beautiful *her*. From the very beginning, we are alive because of a loving, life-giving relationship with our Creator.

I want my grandchildren, my special gifts, to know by the way I love them that they are not only significant and highly valued by Grandpa but also by God who made them! It is important to remember this. As they get on with this adventure of living, certain situations and even some people will try to destroy that sense of their true value. I want to help them remember that God's opinion is the only one that counts. He thinks they are beautiful.

DEAR FATHER,

I pray that You help my wonderful grandchildren to always embrace their value and significance. Whenever circumstances or people tell them that they are no good or treat them disrespectfully—even abusively—help them stand up on the inside. Let my grandchildren hear Your voice telling them, "I created you. You are precious to Me." Give them the strength to hold on to Your opinion and not be intimidated or tricked by anyone else's. I pray that my dear grandchildren will always be in a loving relationship with You and continue to receive Your kiss of life. Amen.

You made all the delicate, inner parts of my body
   and knit me together in my mother's womb.
Thank you for making me so wonderfully complex!
   Your workmanship is marvelous.

PSALM 139:13-14

A Loving Friend

George Eliot's famous poem beautifully captures the essence of a loving relationship.

> *Oh, the comfort, the inexpressible comfort of feeling safe with a person;*
> *having neither to weigh thoughts nor to measure words but pouring*
> *them all right out, just as they are, chaff and grain together, certain*
> *that a faithful hand will take and sift them, keep what is worth keep-*
> *ing, and then, with the breath of kindness, blow the rest away.*

I was twelve years old, living in a small Colorado town, and had made a wonderful friend, the closest friend I ever had in my short life. We were insepa-rable. We walked to and from school together, played on the track and football teams together, and skated on the frozen irrigation canals, icy highways winding through the sprawling fields.

Then without warning, work ran out, money ran out, and food started to run out. Suddenly uprooted, my family moved two thousand miles away to Washing-ton state, so my dad could start a new job. Even now I remember the hurt I felt when I realized my friend and I would never see each other again. Though we promised we'd stay connected somehow, we both knew we couldn't. As I sat in the back of our car, wedged between the boxes and sacks containing our few belong-ings, I vowed, "I will never make a close friend ever again. It hurts too much to leave them."

Though I did not keep the vow, that little twelve-year-old boy had started learning how deep and precious friendships can be. As we spend our lives thirsting for a safe, loving friend, we can come upon so many disappointments—our own failures or another's inability to fulfill a hopeful expectation. The rising hope is overshadowed by pain.

Grandparents are in a unique position to provide friendship—a lifelong friendship. There are no parental demands or prohibitions, particularly concerning the cookies and candies, which are always plentiful at Papa and Gram's. We have the luxury of doling out our undivided attention to our grandchildren and even (whisper it) spoiling them. Grandparents can be the first to grant "the comfort, the inexpressible comfort of feeling safe with a person."

In this safety our grandchildren not only experience a deep, lifelong friendship, but they also learn the beautiful art of being a true friend.

A friend is always loyal, and a brother is
born to help in time of need.
PROVERBS 17:17

DEAR HEAVENLY FATHER,

Grant me the patience to be a place of safety for my grandchildren. Grant me the peace to be a place of comfort. Grant me the wisdom to see that grain of value or the emptiness of chaff. Help me never blow away the grain of our friendship. Amen.

Loving Friend

A real friend sticks
closer than a brother.

PROVERBS 18:24

Memorials

As our children were growing up, they were fortunate to have their grandparents living close by. My mom and dad were superb storytellers. They had an unlimited supply of tales—stories about fishing, hunting, traveling, and surviving hard times—and they told them often. A few were even accompanied by old songs. I loved those old stories, and I loved that Mom and Dad were telling them to their grandchildren. I noticed the slight embellishments every now and then, but grandparents—and storytellers—have permission to do that.

One of our favorite stories was about my grandfather, who lived a life rich in regards to story material, most of which needed no embellishment. The tales about his years as a rough and rowdy Montana railroader were filled with the stuff that makes great novels. The best story, though, did not come from those years. This story was about his sixtieth year. That year he came to a transforming faith in God and was completely changed. No more fighting and carousing for him! In fact, he sensed God calling him to be an evangelist. Considering he had only a third-grade education, that was quite a stretch. Despite the obstacles, he returned to his boyhood roots in rural Wisconsin, started holding meetings in some of the country churches, and eventually became a pastor of one of the town's community churches.

I asked Dad, "Did you ever hear him preach?"

"Once," he said.

"How was it?"

He smiled and then answered, "Well, what he lacked in content he made up for in volume."

Grandpa's story of God's grace and forgiveness was welcomed. His simple, though loud, preaching brought hope to those people.

I remember Grandpa through those stories. Though we met only once when I was just an infant, he greatly influenced my life. A few years ago, I had the opportunity to go to his small hometown on the banks of the Mississippi River. With help from the locals who had actually heard of him, I found the small, well-kept cemetery on the hill outside of town overlooking the beautiful dairy land. I knelt beside a tombstone that read: "Elmer Cook, Evangelist." It was not only a memorial to my grandfather, but more importantly, a lasting monument to the transforming power of a strong faith in God.

As grandparents, we are not only telling a story, we are becoming a story. The story laces the generations together. Tell and live it carefully for it will shape the young minds of our grandchildren long after we are gone.

We will use these stones to build a memorial. In the future your children will ask you, "What do these stones mean?" Then you can tell them, "They remind us that the Jordan River stopped flowing when the Ark of the Lord's Covenant went across." These stones will stand as a memorial among the people of Israel forever.

Joshua 4:6-7

LOVING AND GRACIOUS FATHER,

Your love and faithfulness are forever imprinted on every page of my life. There are so many memorials that illustrate Your love and hope. As I tell my grandchildren about those memorials, I pray they will better understand my faith in You. I also pray as the story of my life is woven into their memories, new memorials of Your faithfulness and love will be erected. Amen.

The Grand Piano

I was nine years old when my parents enrolled me in a one-week summer vacation Bible school. Each day we memorized a verse from the Bible so that on Friday we could stand up and recite one of these verses in front of everybody. The verses were just short sentences or phrases, and I knew all of them, but the thought of standing in front of all those kids terrified me! I had a full-blown case of stage fright at nine years old.

On the stage in front of me, a grand piano sat behind a little curtain. In a panic, I jumped up and slid under that piano. Suddenly and to my horror, a teacher climbed under the piano with me.

"What are we doing here?" he whispered.

"I don't know what you're doing, but I'm hiding," I whispered back.

"Why are you hiding?"

"Because I'm afraid to say my verse," I confessed as the tears started running down my cheeks.

To my surprise, he didn't drag me back to my seat but began to tell me about Jesus who could help me with all my fears. In perfect nine-year-old language, he helped me ask Jesus to come into my heart and be with me for all my life. That teacher told me the truth. Jesus heard the terrified little boy under the grand piano. He has been with me now for over sixty years.

You don't have to be nine years old and lying in panic under a piano to ask Jesus to join you in life. Any age, any posture, any reason will do.

Our world is a dangerous place for children. They must not be left alone to fend for themselves. The greatest gift we can give our grandchildren is the example of a life lived in concert with our heavenly Father. Every child deserves a godly grandparent who is willing to crawl under the grand piano with them. Grandma and I pray regularly for our children, grandchildren, and great-grandchildren. Our most constant prayer is that they will keep their hearts open to Jesus and follow His leadership throughout life. You see, Grandpa learned more than sixty years ago how true this promise is.

In my desperation I prayed, and
the Lord listened;
he saved me from all my troubles.

Psalm 34:6

Dear Jesus,

I pray my grandchildren know how precious they are and how much You love them. May they open their lives to You and allow You to join them, help them, and lead them into the future You have for them. When fearful, difficult, or even dangerous things happen, hold them close and give them courage. You have been faithful to me these many years. I know You will be faithful to them as well. Amen.

Dreams

"What do you want to be when you grow up?" Every child has heard that question and tried to answer it before he even had a clue what it meant.

"Fireman."

"Doctor."

"President."

They have great dreams that change several times between sunup and sundown.

I listen to those dreams and sometimes even join you in the dreaming, my dear grandchild, and…I wonder. I wonder not only about what dream you will pursue and what you will choose to be, but I also wonder who you will listen to on the journey. Who will influence and guide you along the way? What seemingly insignificant decision will you make that opens up an entirely new path and gives you a surprising new dream? A hunch, a word, an unexpected friendship, they all bring unforeseen twists and turns in the road.

People—family, teachers, even strangers, most of them well-meaning—sometimes want to use you to reach their own dreams, caring little about yours. It can seem like everybody loves you and has a wonderful plan for your life. There are so many voices. How will you figure it out? Who will win your attention?

In all this static, there is a voice that I want you to hear. It is the voice of God. His is the most important. His is usually the only one not screaming at you. In fact, His is called the "still small voice." Gently, almost in a whisper, He speaks to your heart. He really does love you and is the One who knows you best. He understands your hopes and dreams. In fact, He has even given you some of them. He knows what will give you meaning and bring you joy. He can steer you in the right direction because He really does have a wonderful plan for your life, a plan that fits with the way He has created you. If you respond to His voice, He will lead you in the right paths.

Family, teachers, and friends, they all can have valuable things to say, good suggestions, and sometimes great insight. Listen to what they are saying but weigh everything against His voice, against His plan. Sometimes other voices can help you hear His better. He alone comes to you from the future—your future. Everyone else comes to you from your past and present. God comes to guide you into a future that He already understands. If you learn to listen on the inside, He will always show you the next step to take.

"For I know the plans I have for you," says the LORD. "They are plans for good and not for disaster, to give you a future and a hope."
JEREMIAH 29:11

Trust in the LORD with all your heart;

do not depend on your own understanding.

Seek his will in all you do,

and he will show you which path to take.

PROVERBS 3:5-6

DEAR LORD,

I know You have a wonderful future for my grandchildren. It's a future more awesome than they could design by themselves and one that includes their dreams and goes far beyond them all. I pray You will protect them from the voices and influences that might hurt them, voices that would turn them from Your pathways. May their hearts always be soft and sensitive to Your whispers. Teach me to be gentle with their dreams, to neither impose my own dreams nor crush theirs. Help me show them how to acknowledge You and how to listen with their heart. I pray that I will always make it easier for them to hear Your whispers. Amen.

Living with Gratitude

It's so easy to be discontented with the way things are, with what we have or don't have.

"I wish..."

"If only..."

"I can't wait until..."

We dream about the past or wish into the future and miss today. We are encouraged on every side to believe that more of something or someplace else would be better. We are bombarded from every direction until we become addicted to the demands. Bigger! Newer! Faster! Prettier!

I don't want to go there and certainly don't want my grandchildren to stumble down that path. I don't want them to be so focused on what they don't have that they miss what they have right now. I want my grandchildren to understand where this appetite for stuff comes from.

When my son Jamie was 13 years old, he came with me on a trip to Hong Kong. Though that great city holds many beautiful sights, tragedies can be found there too. One afternoon Jamie went with a group of people to one of the refugee camps not far from where we were staying. He met a young man about his same age. This boy invited my son to come and see where he lived. Jamie followed him to a tiny, cage-like enclosure in one of the warehouse dorms.

When he returned, my son explained, "It looked like a rabbit hutch, Dad. He didn't have anything. He was teaching himself to speak English from some comic books he'd found. Everything he had was in that cage. He wasn't bitter or angry about having nothing. In fact, Dad, I think he was happier than me, and I have just about everything."

I brought a very different son home from that trip. True, he was still a teenager and liked his stuff, but he never forgot that boy. I believe that memory played a part in his decision years later to spend two years in Africa with the Peace Corps. He and his wife lived in a remote village with people who had very little and children who had been orphaned because of the AIDS epidemic.

Even though they now live in the States, neither Jamie nor his wife is driven by a need for stuff. They are very grateful for everything they have. Maybe that's the secret! By living life with an attitude of gratitude, we can be thankful for where we are, what we have, and even who we are.

My dear grandchild, I want you to learn of this secret. I don't want discontent to rob you of the here and now. Granted, it might seem nice to have more things or be in a different place, but if a little boy living in a "rabbit hutch" in a refugee camp can be grateful, I guess you and I can learn to live our lives with gratitude.

Loving Father,

I thank You so much for my wonderful grandchildren. I pray that as they grow, they will experience the great joy of Your presence every minute of every day. Protect them from an addiction to stuff or comfort. I pray they will learn to live gratefully and confidently. I pray that my influence will help them understand that You are present, and because of that, they can live with gratitude, even when the circumstances aren't the best. Help me be an illustration of one who gives thanks in all circumstances. Amen.

Be thankful in all circumstances, for this is
God's will for you who belong to Christ Jesus.

1 Thessalonians 5:18

The Smiling God

Let's pretend that one day the doorbell rings. It surprises you because you are not expecting anyone. You open the door, and standing there on your porch is God! I don't know how you know it is God; you just do.

Now let me ask you a question. As He looks at you, what is the expression on His face? (I know it's far-fetched, but that's the fun part of imagining something.)

Is He stern and intense? Is He frowning? Does He look angry? And why is He at your door? What have you done that would require God to make a house call?

This little pretend story can help us understand what our God is like and what He thinks of us. We like God, but we are not sure He likes us. We tend to make Him into our most important authority figure. He's the megacop, the all-knowing sheriff in the sky, the cosmic, angry parent who is looking for a reason to punish us, and He sure doesn't have to look very hard.

Let's pretend a little more. This is how I imagine Him to be when I open the door and see Him standing there. He has a big smile on His face, and before I can do anything, He steps forward and gives me a great big hug. He immediately says, "I'm so glad you are home. I love you so much! I wanted to come by to just enjoy being with you for a while. May I come in?"

After what seems like a really short time, but actually has been several hours, He gets up to leave. I want Him to stay. In fact, I wish He would move in and live with me forever. This has been a most wonderful time. We have laughed and cried together. I have never in my whole life been more comfortable with anyone. It's as if we belonged together, like we were made for each other.

Well, my dear grandchild, though this story is imaginary, the God that I have told you about is not. He really does love you. He thoroughly enjoys and accepts you. You really do belong together. He is actually smiling and has a twinkle in His eyes as He looks at you.

Please remember that God is neither a megacop nor a cosmic parent glaring at you or disapproving of you. You see, Jesus is God up close. He said, "If you have seen me, you have seen the Father." Jesus is God in three dimensions. People loved Him. They begged to be with Him. They invited Him into their homes and to their celebrations. Even little children like you ran to be with Him. He often held them in His arms and blessed them. He always welcomed them and warned people not to hurt them.

You know, my dear, He and I have walked together for many years, and I know He is wonderful! He is loving! He is smiling! If you look with your heart-eyes, you too will see Him smiling at you with a twinkle in His eyes and a welcome on His lips.

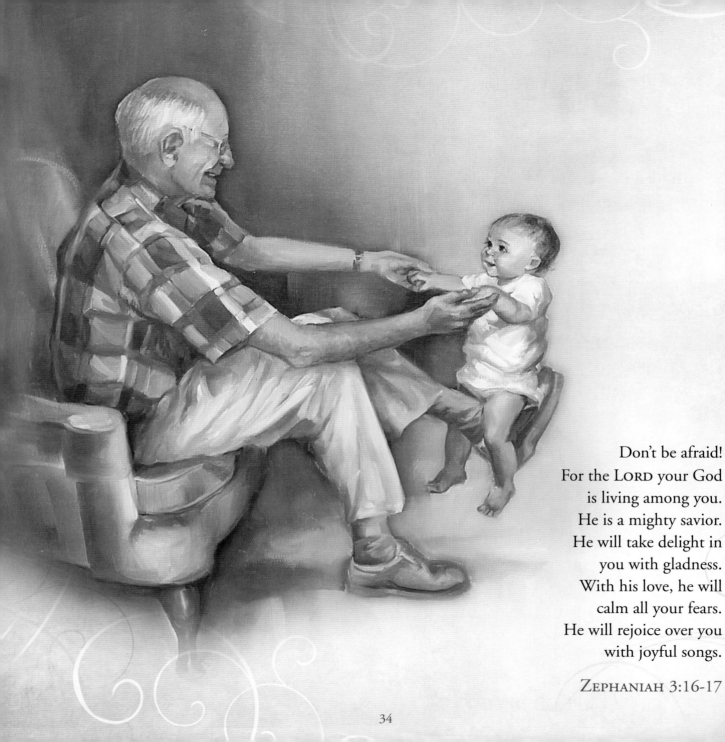

Don't be afraid!
For the LORD your God
is living among you.
He is a mighty savior.
He will take delight in
you with gladness.
With his love, he will
calm all your fears.
He will rejoice over you
with joyful songs.

ZEPHANIAH 3:16-17

LOVING FATHER,

You are so wonderful. Help my dear grandchildren understand that. I pray they never confuse You with the angry and offensive people who want to hurt them. Like the children in the Bible stories, may they run to You and be held in Your arms. Let them see that You are always on their side and against anyone or anything that might keep them from You or make them think You don't approve of them. I pray they will always see Your smile and the twinkle of pride in Your eyes as You look at them. I pray that I will make it easy for them to know how much You love and accept them by the way I welcome them into my own arms and heart. Amen.

God's Masterpiece

Many years ago I was at the Louvre, a great museum in Paris. It is filled with treasures of all kinds. With all there was to see, I wanted to be sure to find Venus de Milo, the famous Greek sculpture. I was directed to an enormous hall filled with marvelous sculptures by great masters. Venus de Milo was the queen. She held court in her special place. Her subjects crowded around to admire her. She was pure white and smooth as satin. Everyone was in awe of her. No one even spoke in her presence. She had us spellbound. We almost expected her to speak.

I spent that wonderful day walking amongst the masterpieces. I was captivated by the beauty and humbled by the remarkable craftsmanship. It was a day I will never forget.

As incredible as these great treasures are, you, my dear grandchild, are far more wonderful, far more valuable. You see, the Bible tells us that you are God's special work of art. As you allow Him to walk with you and guide you, He will carefully and artfully shape you. He uses each experience—both good and difficult—like a brush in His magnificent hand to make you into a masterpiece. The Master carefully shapes a unique you...a beautiful you...a strong and gifted you. Because He comes from your future, He is able to shape every detail of your life so you will fit perfectly into the wonderful destiny He has for you. He takes those things that were intended to destroy you and turns them into a benefit.

Venus de Milo did not become a masterpiece only after she was completed. She was a masterpiece when she was but a vision in the master's mind. The artist saw her in the rough stone he chose and transformed that rock into the beautiful figure he had seen.

God, the great Master, sees all you can be. If you let Him, He will make that vision a reality. But remember, you are not a masterpiece only after you are finished. You are a treasure the moment the Master begins His work and every moment along the way.

> For we are God's masterpiece.
> He has created us anew in Christ Jesus,
> so we can do the good things he planned for us long ago.
>
> EPHESIANS 2:10

HEAVENLY FATHER,

Thank You for this precious treasure You have brought into my life. Help my grandchildren see that they are a treasure not just to me, but most importantly, to You. No matter what happens, You are always creating, forming, and shaping them. I pray they will allow You to work in their lives. Even when circumstances are difficult or confusing, help them remember they are Your wonderful works of art. I pray that You will help me remember that too. I pray I will always encourage my grandchildren to trust You. May I treat them with care. Help me never lose sight of the wonderful fact that they are a valuable, one-of-a-kind work of art and treasure them. Amen.

You Are Safe with God

Have you ever noticed how often God gets credit for the bad and luck gets credit for the good?

A terrible earthquake once caused homes and businesses to drop out of sight. The earth seemed to open up and swallow them. One family was the one exception. They were not injured, and their home was untouched except for some broken china. Not even a window was cracked. In fact, that home became a shelter for dozens of neighbors during the difficult days that followed. Though all the devastation was considered an "act of God," the family whose home was saved was considered *lucky*.

When a little boy survived a terrible disease, which was considered nearly always fatal, he was called "one of the lucky ones." After another child died of the same disease, the grieving parents tried to make sense of one of the statements the pastor made at the funeral. It was supposed to be comforting. He had explained, "God needed another little angel in heaven." The parents wondered, *How are we supposed to love a God who has torn our precious baby from our arms because He needs another angel? Why couldn't our son have been "one of the lucky ones"?*

After a series of disappointing losses, a tortured person is advised that God is just trying to teach her a lesson. The adviser, however, is never quite sure what the lesson is. Of course, God doesn't tell her either. He just keeps "teaching" and causing more confusion.

Can we really trust a God who would indiscriminately kill and maim innocent people and destroy everything they have? Is it really better to be lucky? Where do grieving parents go for comfort if God is responsible for the death of their child? Is God really such an incompetent teacher that He has to resort to pain, loss, or disappointment to teach us some lesson He won't even explain?

I want my grandchildren to understand that the God whom Grandpa loves and trusts is not like that. I want them to know that no matter what they are experiencing, they can go to God and be assured that He will help them and keep them safe. They must understand that He is always on their side. God is never on the side of their troubles.

When I was receiving treatment for cancer, I was completely confident my doctors were on my side and never on the side of the cancer. I felt safe going to them because they were my healers; they were not the cause of my disease. If I know that fact about my doctors, I certainly know it to be true about my God, who is called the "great physician." Our God is great because He is always our healer, never our torturer. David, the famous king of Israel, wrote, "I will say of the Lord, 'He is my refuge and my fortress, my God, in whom I trust'" (Psalm 91:2 NIV).

That's the God I want you, my grandchildren, to know. He is the *only* God. There is no mean, angry God out there looking to hurt you. You are not all alone. You don't need to hope that luck will help you. God is predictably good and deeply in love with you. When things get scary, you can hear Him say, "Don't be afraid for I am with you."

I love you so much! I wish I could be with you whenever life gets difficult or frightening, but, sadly, no matter how much I want to, I can't. I will, however, help you know the God who loves you in ways even Grandpa can't. He is always with you, so you won't have to be alone or afraid. You can live with courage and confidence because this God—our God—gives you strength and helps you when you ask, just like He did for David and just like He has done for me.

God is our refuge and strength, an
ever-present help in trouble.

Psalm 46:1 niv

Safe with God

GRACIOUS FATHER,

Thank You for Your goodness and Your faithfulness. You have certainly been my refuge and help in every time of trouble. I am sorry for the false ideas and accusations that are said about You. I pray that my grandchildren will not be influenced by them, even when they come from seemingly well-meaning people. Help them to trust You. May they know they are always safe with You because You are in love with them, You willingly help them, and You certainly would never harm them. I pray they will invite You to join them in every minute of their lives. Let them experience the confidence, courage, and strength that come from Your presence. Help me accurately reflect Your goodness and love to them. I pray they will experience a safe and loving grandfather so they can more easily experience a safe and loving heavenly Father. Amen.

Growing Young

The Bible says some surprising things about children. For example, Jesus didn't suggest that children grow up and become like adults. He said that adults should grow young and become like children.

In the Bible (Mark 10:13-15), one of Jesus' best friends tells us of a time when the disciples were trying to keep the children away from Jesus. Believing the children were misbehaving and bothering Jesus, they scolded the parents and tried to shoo the children away. When Jesus saw what was going on, "he was angry with his disciples" and rebuked them. Then Jesus lovingly welcomed the children with opened arms and blessed them. On another occasion, Jesus sternly reprimanded those who would harm "one of these little ones" or cause them to lose faith (Mark 9:42).

This picture of Jesus opening His arms and embracing the children is powerful! It gives us a striking view into the heart of God. In fact, Jesus says unless we adults become like these believing children, we can't become part of His kingdom.

As a grandfather, this brings two things into sharp focus for me. The first is that I must never forget that my grandchildren are some of the little ones Jesus was talking about. We grandparents must always encourage that simple faith. We must never weaken or inhibit our grandchildren's belief but rather guard and value it as God's special deposit into their lives. We want them to understand how much Jesus loves and welcomes them. We are their advocates against the voices that try to keep them away from Him and cause them to doubt and question. We are to bring our grandchildren to Jesus' open arms so that they might experience His blessing.

The second important point for us as grandparents is to let our grandchildren lead us to God's kingdom. We must learn from their simple trust, unvarnished love, spontaneous joy, and unlimited curiosity.

We have developed into sophisticated and guarded adults. We are partial and judgmental when we dole out our love—even to our friends. Too often we've rushed our faith from our heart to our head. It has become diluted by our mature logic. But these wonderful children go directly to our heart, and if we let them, they will coax our faith back to its original, uncomplicated condition.

It is easy to get wrapped up in teaching them all the great things we have learned about being an adult and fail to learn from them the art of becoming a believing child.

"Let the children come to me. Don't stop them! For the Kingdom of God belongs to those who are like these children..." Then he took the children in his arms and placed his hands on their heads and blessed them.

MARK 10:14,16

DEAR JESUS,

Give me wisdom as I seek to love my grandchildren and help them love You. More than anything I want them to be safe in Your arms and receive Your blessing. Grant that my words, acts, and attitudes increase their belief in You. And, Lord, help me learn how to be a believing child from them. I pray that my old head will not keep me from having a child's heart and that I may enter Your kingdom with my grandchildren. Amen.

A child's eyes, those clear, wells of
undefiled thought—
What on earth can be more beautiful?
Full of hope, love and curiosity,
they meet your own.
In prayer, how earnest;
In joy, how sparkling;
In sympathy, how tender!

CAROLINE NORTON

The plans of the LORD stand firm forever,
the purposes of his heart through all generations.

PSALM 33:11 NIV

So deep in my soul
the still prayer of devotion,
Unheard by the world,
rises silent to Thee.

THOMAS MOORE

Gentle Jesus, Meek and Mild

Gentle Jesus, meek and mild,
Look upon a little child;
Pity my simplicity,
Suffer me to come to Thee.

Lamb of God, I look to Thee;
Thou shalt my Example be;
Thou art gentle, meek, and mild;
Thou wast once a little child.

Loving Jesus, gentle Lamb,
In Thy gracious hands I am;
Make me, Savior, what Thou art,
Live Thyself within my heart.

I shall then show forth Thy praise,
Serve Thee all my happy days;
Then the world shall always see
Christ, the holy Child, in me.

Charles Wesley